Ruthless Heaven

poems by

Ian Randall Wilson

Finishing Line Press
Georgetown, Kentucky

Ruthless Heaven

ACKNOWLEDGMENTS

AMP: "Exact Words Are Hard To Live By"; "Ruthless Heaven"; "Three City Blocks"

Peacock Journal: "At 3 A.M."; "Before Swerving"; "Language Waits"

My thanks to the editors of the journals in which some of these poems first appeared.

Grateful appreciation to Gail Wronsky, Tony Hoagland, Dean Young, Jack Grapes
and Heather McHugh, my first teachers of poetry.

To Rick Bursky who reads so much of my work and provides valuable insight and
guidance, not to mention his abiding friendship.

To Peter Levitt who is able to take on the mind of the poet and interrogate each
piece to make it its best self.

To Ron Alexander for his support and guidance.

To my first and most important reader, Denise, who makes it all possible.

Publisher: Leah Maines

Editor: Christen Kincaid

Cover Art: "Lightning Strike Over Field Landscape" © Paul Lampard |
Dreamstime.com

Author Photo: Rebecca Dru

Cover Design: Elizabeth Maines McCleavy

Printed in the USA on acid-free paper.
Order online: www.finishinglinepress.com
               also available on amazon.com

Author inquiries and mail orders:
Finishing Line Press
P. O. Box 1626
Georgetown, Kentucky 40324
U. S. A.

Table of Contents

For Denise

I want to stay on some great rock
And fish forever on and on
—Wang Wei (tr. G.W. Robinson)

BEAUTIFUL LIFE

A marvel discovering myself
unformed ungrounded mostly
ignorant. When I was a boy
I thought there was always
something seriously wrong with me.
I couldn't walk straight
or keep my head up.
Now the uncertainty only returns
when lightning strikes
or the ground shakes.
I have placed detectors
in every room
to give me a few seconds warning
before the earth decides
to shout its next shout.

THE LEAVES

A place in the landscape
for me to spend these last few hours
dictating myself to the world.
All this greenery
and my reluctant pen.

The children next door are shouting.
They run among the trees.
How wonderful to see them
away from their small screens.

After all this time
am I still
not yet known
to myself?

The cat is stalking a local bird.
Three bees sweep by
on their way
to business among the blossoms.
I make one more try
to open the castle of myself.
Emerge into this radiant world.

AFTERWORD

And what about the light
wanted at the moment
the world is balanced
on points of darkness?

An exquisite voice
sings from next door.
The trash pickers rumble
down the alley.

I am packing up her boxes.
I am giving a life away.
All around me air and paper.
What was that sound?
Was something said?
What was it I thought I heard?

UNTIL DEATH

The air is papered with conversation.
We are seated on folding chairs.
The many have traveled
across the vast
to be here.
A landscape beautiful
with cows.

The bride walks the aisle.
An old man coughs
rubs back tears.
Rain, reported to be scattered,
breaks out in sheets.
A ruin of careful hairstyles
also the dress.
The storm is sudden
and gone over
the next slope.

I have a clear view of trees
from the back porch.
I should be here more often.
Everything is moving forward
alone on earth.

GOD IS DYING AT HOME

The other fathers gather
outside in the meadow.
Dancing and drums.
The spirit guides direct
this latest transition.
The yellow light works its way through fog
seeking small rifts in the vapors,
the way to most of us.
Trees, usually fortified with birds,
are empty now, nests vacated.
When the end comes,
there will be no stretching the afterwards
for an extra minute
or even one more blink of sun.

INEVITABLE

It is sunny now
in the world of my creation.
A boy waters the lawn
his dog frolics in the spray.
The flowers grow abundant
swallowing sweetness
in every move of their stems.
Years go by
and age comes slowly
until a message from the afterlife
last escapes our gasping throats.

THE ELEPHANT IS PACING

I don't get home
before the fields succumb to night.
A low wattage bulb
at the widow's door
casts its small cone
in a pretense of welcome.

Hours later I am by the window
considering how the end
might come (one hopes
for the slight exhalation)
as sleep and I continue
our unseasonable relations.

The ones who believe
say it's a glory
going home to him.

What if it's but
a return to air
and soil vast as forever?
The earth will make
at least one new rotation
before I leave where I am
for somewhere else.

DESCENDING

I ignore my current form
by covering mirrors.
Immediately I am reshaped,
resurfaced (and only in a figurative way),
resurrected as a man
with a slight limp into his humanity.
(I'm kind to cats.)

I'm taken hostage
by an elevator.
I am released.
I sit in a room for 10 hours.
The thing inside the thing inside the thing—
a silence allowing me
to say what I'm not.
Then hours more elsewhere.
Repetition. Recollection.
No answers. Many walls.
Thus the 20th century expires.

EXAMINED LIFE

While its cousin
the unexamined might
not be worth living,
the problem is mine
far too scrutinized.

The black songs
of late summer
get sung and sung
until the howl
of the neighbor dogs—
or death now—
might be preferable.

I'm an old man
who takes an hour
to get out
under the old tree.
Don't even think
about asking me to move.

The sun will have to be much hotter
and the hour much later
and my thirst intense
before the earth's rotation
(or you)
can force me
to go inside.

KEEPING LISTS

The morning is remodeled
and those displaced set right.
A new grave. With shipments blocked
the hospital cannot restock its shelves.

3 days without sniper fire
No police have shot anyone else.
We must turn out for every celebration
like pennies falling
from the pockets of a drunk.
The drinks are free
all we need do
is get past the burned-out bank.

We'll be safe
after hours
when the night has its own distinct darkness.
All the little wanderers.
The widowed glass.
It is the moon that betrays us.
We run by the church that was bombed
and the school collapsed.
The particles combine and recombine.
We can't make sense of anything in our tiny lives.

OH FOR KINGS

Burst glass. A story clamoring
for someone to change it.
In a certain light
weather expands. Heat
fragments the day.
A man tries rebuilding the world.
Another harvests water.
No two deaths alike.
The fires of a season ago
were not as large as the ones today.
Our progress measured
by conflagration
guides us into concert
with the ever burning sun.

FADE BEHIND US

What is lost behind roads and churches
a fall night falling
on western lawns.
The sky knuckles over fences.
In the windows of the nearest houses
a choice of waste and ruin:
The flat hand strikes.
Body of a woman bent.
A child cries.
Next door an old man sits
in a yard
his mind has left him.
He underscores the hours
saved for him
with never-ending screams.

ONLY THE CEASELESS

This night a mental desiccation
despite five glasses of ale.
The goggled edge to sky
a replacement for stars.
Damned hills turned swell.
Ground rising up.
Silence shows its judgment
for all infernal deeds.
A hooked jay mocking.
A vacant tree.
Somewhere a path home—
though the moon delays in rising,
and will not let us find it.

GOVERNING WAVES

You may say "No" to a dog
and hope for change.
Unlike the universe
putting up a warning hand.
The plants unveil their abiding link
to the river's bend
in their far-reaching roots.
All connections become visible
and the nine operations of priests
no longer hide behind mesh.
After sky and every atom clears,
the business of the life resumes
and if you have lived through it
you resume, too,
until next time you are called.
The lord overhears all the beautiful grumblers,
their bellies darkening the world.

THE HOUSE

There's a house walking about in the sun,
it ambles toward us in the brilliant yellow.
I have nothing special to do today. The house visits
under the sun like the neighbor dogs in the yard.

When the sun sets the house stops.
We stand outside
quiet as a heartbeat.
Waiting, as everyone does,
for the signal—
the earth to turn
and the night erase.

THE ROAD AND THE FOG

A road moves through us in the fog.
It sprints around in the shifting mists.
It has direction. It knows its path
in the fog like a zealot called to the temple.

When the fog lifts the road veers off
into the great distance, open and beckoning,
calling us to decide:
stay or come along now. Run.

DOMINION

We have entered the last curl
of our extinction.
Let us dance
while spirit guides play.
The commons are filling
with people bursting to know.
Dust clings to our skin
and we trample the early buds.
The children think it is a game
and run about, but the parents
have gotten the idea.
We are digging
no longer able
to see the top.
Soon the earth will engulf us
and grow roses over our heads.

THE TOWN SLEEPS

His life boils up in the coming light.
No—only coffee spilling over.
Hello day.
A new riddle to solve
out back among the ascending trees.

The brothers exchanged enough mail
to lame the postman.
This happened years ago
when they were boys
separated by angry parents.
Now one lies
in the ground
his heart exploded.

The spring is very wet
and the walls are filled to repletion.
Out west, they are dying of thirst,
River beds expose
their crag of mineral bones
and long dumped cars.

Some days the rumor goes
the priests are coming.
Some days soldiers.
He stands by the road,
watches and waits.
The years turns.
The earth passes.
The morning light that used to thrill him
thrills him no longer,
and all the time music plays
from the house next door.

EXACT WORDS ARE HARD TO LIVE BY

I have been trying to reclaim
the things within my reach
according to the shouting fathers
wisdom handed down to successive
generations on television shows.
A child may be innocent
until his parents prove him guilty.
We are stuck in this moment
until we're not
and the sun set drives us
into the river of darkness.

We breathe at the same time.
Other forms of unison are not easy.
The tea turns cloudy.
Grasshoppers arrive
with their messages from the afterlife.
The spirit guides are crushing rocks
in the backyard and beating drums,
inviting the ground to disappear.
Everyone begins to look hard at everyone else.
We are alone under the moon
the century flowing as gravestones reappear
according to the level of the drought.
I hear the voices—the fathers
and a million others talking.
The earth has no one to call.

THE CENTER HAS NO CENTER

The universe of loneliness is everywhere.
Can't cross the street without
its small presence bumping up against me.

Planes begin their rapprochement
with the sky. Bodies glow.
Those oaks drowned in the run-off
from the road
change the definition
of trees.

The man next door,
according to the evening news,
dies obsolete.
I spend the rest of the night
in attempts
to reinvent myself.
Careful where I walk
on a floor littered
with broken riddles.

OCEAN BOTTLES

I walk to while away
the garden of time passing.
For the rest,
it's Thursday.
In the middle of the summer's happy week
I lie down in the dirt,
conduct rehearsals of the future.
Flowers wreath me
and the faint rot
of last year's covered-over plantings.

It's a bullshit age
wouldn't you say?
People let their dogs
foul the streets,
and you, young man with headphones on
head down reading your phone—
the world is here
about to run into you.
You don't like my horn?
Come back from your secret hideout
among the electrons,
give them up
and smell the earth.

RUTHLESS HEAVEN

On this day five years ago,
he is shot near the tree.
God takes no side in this.
The ocean stays pure.
His spirit rises past
the tropic of swallows
beyond the nylon skyline.

At his mother's house
a solitary bulb shines
into the smudge where light
interdicts the dark.
Otherwise the void
casts no shadow.
His room stays empty,
door brilliantly obedient
to its closed nature.

I walk past the flower bed
of he who has departed,
hindered by the memories
no one wants to remember.
Even the world is pretending
that the stone marking
his grave was hewn yesterday.

THREE CITY BLOCKS

Outside the storefront
the light pulls
cold from the wind.
A language
momentarily on the tongue—
the fishmonger and the barber
beat out the rhythms of their day.
Always a grammar in small towns,
the way people try to time themselves
from childhood to old age.
In the town square
dissidents gather
only to be repelled
by the guard.
A dog snaps.
A woman screams.
Blood throbs atop concrete.
We had thought
the world would welcome us.
How soon we discover
the other hand is never waiting.

COMBAT ZONE

A golden note breaks over the forest,
then drummers become busy
dispensing courage into the fog.
In the time before the first shot
a bird trills,
the wind makes the branches wave.
After this fight has ended
after the next and the next,
the dead will bury themselves,
and the living will soon join them—
only earth will be itself, unforgiving.

MOMENTS BETWEEN DREAMING AND WAKING

Life has one solution
cannot be undone.
One finish.
Inevitable turn.

Waves come before grief,
before the night distorts our sense
of here and after,
when we still believe
he is upstairs sleeping,
not moldering
in the field
three towns over.

Every night treetops turn violet,
sky a mirror of the concluding day.
Something should be shared.
Something should be said.
Words go here.

THE MIND IS ANYTHING

I live as if death
were three weeks away.
Still time
to cut some flowers
take in
the wash,
clear
the streaky windows
and put out food for the cat.
In the meantime,
any last requests?

IN THE HOUSE WHERE EVERYTHING CHANGES

Another morning
where trees sweep and swing.
A crazy wind outside
carrying desert heat.
Trunks a heavy body,
branches bones for leaves.
I am marked by tremor.
Muscles rigid.
Shadows wander the room.
The laws of momentum force me on.
If I were in charge,
I would rewrite the laws of stoppage.
No bodies in motion without my permit.
I would like to do nothing. To halt.
Instead, everything expands in time
toward its conclusion.
Gusts rattling coats.
The resplendent usual progressing.
Fingertips ablaze at noon.
I am gleaming and the house sees me.
The light reaches its crescendo
explodes all over the ground.
I open a map and unfold separateness.
Me, a member of the carbon universe
whom the earth has disappointed.
The universe must disappoint me
nor can God be trusted to deliver.

LOVERS SEEKING THE BANISHED

Darkness spreads over the lake.
Air parsed into discrete calls:
the loon first and last crying out.
All the chimneys
on all the cabins
devoid of their usual business practices.
Wind searches for a partner.
The builders of old have vanished
remembered by a single small plaque.
Night is said to be passing through the county
touching hillocks and the other glacial formations
the earth let lie for a million years.

NO TALKING MUSIC INTO JOY

I passed through childhood oarless
moved by the family's rudder bones.
As a young man
this cover removed
the river became wide,
its bottom treacherous and obscured.

Now the fog rolls in
My neighbor's wife hopes for a pair of earrings.
In the house on the other side, the children
are straightening teeth.
A population of car washers.
An entire city devoted to summer spectation.

All the planetary bodies
are in motion.
All the possibilities of the universe
in the night sky.
Wait, the river has narrowed.
The passage appears to be ending.
What remains can be stuffed in a teacup.
On the river bank
the blue flowers bloom.

STRAY NARRATIVES

Once burned forest,
its necklace
of green restored.
Took many years.
The mind gone dumb
in its efforts to understand
the Beloved's departure.
Ghosts of the lovers we were
dance in the distance.
The summer house has been sold
and the jewelry divided.
One of us kept the books.
The other the records.
Our secret life is secret no more,
yet for this,
and other more natural destructions,
the earth offers no further detail.

A LIFE FOR OURSELVES

In the marketplace of the heart
a reticent soul does not prosper.
That arena has stood empty for years.
Protesters having pulled up the pavers
for something to throw.
Many are dead—
many more will die.
Yet the countryside rebounds
after each desecration
and the seasons continue
on the only earth we know.

A DAY THROUGH MINUTES

Today my annual pilgrimage
to what's left
of the woods by the shore,
all the new houses in place of ancient trees.
Car time fragmenting life time—
my steady forward pace.
There are lives behind the walls I pass,
but do not confuse a younger love with old.

Everywhere I go, the mutterings of strangers
interrupt my thinking.
After picking over the bones of the morning,
the featured speaker has stopped speaking.
The buzz of cicadas fills the empty air.

Even this long after the recent floods,
caskets in disarray,
relatives disinterred
in the family graveyard.
All of us hoping
for a return to earth.

I have not lingered for months
under the marine layer's gray edge.
Every morning I arrive at the beach
only to turn around and venture home.

THE DEBUNKING

We seek the barking
forms of love.
Rat terriers to greet us.
A white house signals
preoccupations.
Walkway strewn with leaves.
On unsuspecting lawns
the sky practices its theories
of the rise of nation states
in the 20th century.
Altostratus clouds close down
further conversation.
Shuffles at the end of the drive.
A drop and bend for the evening paper,
pages squeaking with news.
The bells are shameless
as wind rises in accompaniment.
We cannot see any of this
from our 2nd floor aerie
convinced the earth is there beneath us
with no one else
to tell us we're wrong.

NATIONS ADVANCE

A minute of hand joy.
One smile. One look
of perturbation.
The dead are laughing
at this most recent reproof.
At 20, time moved
faster than a mirror sent back its news.
I could have been a dozen people
in an afternoon.
At 70, the doorbell sounds
and I have to think
about answering.
Math in mind is cruel at night,
summing up the years still left.
That declivity out back
was once a mountain.
Even the largest earth formations
are ground down
given penitence,
wind, water, wait.

TURPITUDE IN THE FACE OF WHAT'S COMING

The little puppet in my chest
grows a mood.
All the data streaming
from aberrant nerves.
I'm saying my life is not
the lilacs of my parents.
The breeze has abdicated.
Reality does not enjamb.
At this moment the clouds
make a cynical appearance.
They pretend they are concerned
though they hover atop the least
most important place on earth
and spew.

THAT WAS A MOMENT

I step out of the pantry
of my imagination.
A self-portrait drawn by birds.
The merciful is random.
The kelp grows in a particular pattern.

I have asked the prognosticators
for the date of my death.
They have given me three possible days
suggest I select the best
and get back to them.

SIGNS

The old men speak of Death
as if it were a friendly guest.
Ignored is Death's contempt
for language. To say
she has passed
cannot encompass
the emptiness of houses,
sagging beds,
the mirror now
devoid of her reflection.

SCALE

The bed like the deck
of a sinking ship.

Clouds rolling over.
Neighbor dogs first
to warn.

Tectonic plates separating.
The earth expanded.

Houses
used to be.

THE POTTER'S LAMENT

People do not like my pots.
Poor coloration, difficult
textures—some disdain
their shape.
I have made my pots
using elements of wind,
sometimes a touch of earth.
I have thrown a pot
this afternoon
though the world does not wait
for one more pot of mine.
The problem is the pot
comes apart in my hands—
reality on one side,
attempts at beauty
on the other.
I am throwing one more pot
this afternoon expecting it
to join the other pots thrown
in the storage shed outside,
a record of the world, finite, discarded.

ONCE AND SO FORTH

At the bottom of the driveway
words tense.
The light of day
about to be extinguished.
Screams in monosyllables
birds understand.
The neighbor cat
stalking about high grass.
I'd like to put a fence
around the year,
razor it from the calendar.
The night beings
with their own exposition.
Trees a deep-drawn breath
like everywhere on earth
you hear these things.

FOUNDATIONS AND WALLS

The silence in a staircase—
five flights down is plenty of time
for a beautiful forgetting. I yearn for it.
Outside the night being
its own exposition,
a west of cold,
private mausoleum in disrepair.
I walked home under a sail.
The moon conspicuous
for its absence.
Streetlights billowed in the fog.
What are the causes
that set the heart aflame?
I set out to change the world
of expectations. That was
another universe.

CHILDHOOD

Outside my door
grass old
as time intended.

A man leaves.
A woman cries
at memory most unloyal.

The dazzling air erased itself,
returns to primal silence.
The earth would sigh if capable.

ALL GAMES IMAGINED

A night of basic screaming
from the corner house.
Tonight's ambulance flooding darkness
with red flashing.

For some no tasting calm,
compulsion over breath.
Things always go wrong.

I sat by the window.
I believe I slept.
In the morning, street
same as any other
in our small part
of the world.

DEVICES

By all the distant measures—
the heart gap tool,
lost love indicator—
an inexplicable me
springs forth
in the heavy rains.
Ignore my utterances
at those times.
Let the afternoon pass
in reluctant silence.
When order is restored
to the world at large,
I will join you
in the living room
and we will go on living.

LANGUAGE BENDS

In my 50s I stopped
tracking statistics
of the beneficial imperfections.
Oh, the weight creeps up but
enough trouble with the currencies
getting out of bed in the morning.

The oak-solid years touch one
about the waist.
No more dancing
with the abandonment
of fleas.

A long night of listening,
watching, waiting.
At first light
outside the window,
huge unknown shapes
resolve themselves
into a topiary garden
of trim green pigs.
About them mountains and trees.
The earth arrives.

HOW BIRDS SPEND THEIR TIME

The rain goes acoustic this afternoon
brings an audible contraction to my experience.
I know what matters.
A viewing of the frescoes on her back.

An old woman dusts off her sleeves,
tries to put aside
worried thoughts.
The ancestral revelation,

The earth does not respond to anyone's situation.
Go outside and see—
the mountains have not changed
neither has the lake.

SUSPENDED SOUL

A ferocious afternoon of bad ideas
and loose utterances.
The wind rises making the trees
seem shaken by ghosts.
This is not the spring of our fathers
or their fathers.
Happiness appears to have left the century
along with most of the wild life
peculiar to my back yard.
A blast of grief
or an early dinner—
either way no
satisfaction in left-overs

DRAMA VOICE

No words can equalize the continuum.
The men around the field
come from the hustler class
selling the stuff
of their badly conceived rackets.
All week the river has been rising.
Its banks sundered and banks no more.
No containing the anxious reader.
No containing the waters of the damned.
The night is full of holes.
The lunar seas inundate us.

EXPERT AT INTERVIEWING PEOPLE

Here is a man running.
It means something.
For a year the same man running.
What can it mean?
He runs the back roads
and the fields every day
at the same time
and the same pace
no matter if the sun blazes
or the season's rains descend.
This is not my invention,
my way of whipping myself
for my own lack
of staying power.
He's getting older
with each lap,
that much I see.
He runs
and I survive
and in this way
we are equals here on earth.

AT 3 A.M.

This late I am shedding excess
principles along with the trash.
I stepped on something spiny
limped back to the open door.

I await the next stage of my life
all of us reclining in our chairs.
Somewhere armies confront their identical
selves on the next great battlefield.

The windows are incompletely closed.
The door rattles in the wind.
Now is the time when the darkness
issues its invitation for animals
to express themselves
in ways they never knew how.

BEFORE SWERVING

An assembly of the extinguished
in the cemetery across the road.
My home watches over them.
Not the best location,
but the sale price was right.

The dead redefine themselves
in our shifting memory.
The faithful antecedents
cannot be trusted
after all the pictures burn.

We are renting time
as the covering of our souls
reveals itself as something quite thin.
On a scale I can't aspire to
the morning favors me today
letting through a little sun
and heat—the calmness
before the storm.

LANGUAGE WAITS

This is not Spain.
This is not a photograph of Spain.
The intersection has changed
since the last time I visited.

The eucalyptus trees are gone
replaced by concrete pylons
topped with stars.

The metaphors are quarreling
and I am standing by.
I am waiting
for them to hand me
the image I will use
to continue my life.

I am hoping
for ash to sing,
some open organism
living in the cold light.
I may get space
and earth spinning—
nothing more.

Ian Randall Wilson has published two chapbooks, *Theme of the Parabola* and *The Wilson Poems,* both from Hollyridge Press. His fiction, poetry and essays have appeared in many journals including *The Gettysburg Review, The New Mexico Humanities Review, Alaska Quarterly Review, The Mid-American Review,* and *North American Review.* He has an MFA in Fiction and in Poetry from Warren Wilson College. He is on the fiction faculty at the UCLA Extension. By day, he is an executive at Sony Pictures Entertainment.